Free Blog Topics Download!
Not Very Creative or just looking for a list of go to type of articles? Go to http://www.jeremiahboehner.com/content-ideas-for-businesses/ and enter your e-mail and you'll get a free download of over 35 Blog Topics you can use on your blog right away and get Jeremiah Boehner. More Than 60 Ultra Hot Resources to Help You Develop Kick-Butt Idea's For Your Blog!

Introduction:
Content creation is difficult. The constant need to find unique and creative things to discuss can be exhausting for any writer, but you don't need to bang your head against the wall trying to come up with super original, 'no one has ever thought of it before,' content. Inspiration can come from a variety of different places. I've put together this list of resources to help you discover, as well as validate your content ideas. These resources have proven to be incredibly useful for many bloggers, as well as myself, when it comes to sparking ideas and finding strong material for quality blog posts. I've also put together a list of highly recommended tools to help you be a more effective content creator. Please send me a tweet at @sfboehner if you feel this list is missing anything.

About Me:

I've been blogging in some way since 2002 back when blogs were called E-zines. Since then I've started two music-marketing companies, an online music shop, a guerrilla marketing company, and now a digital media company. I'm also currently the head of sales at Mylikes, one of the largest content recommendation networks on the planet. We leverage your content and the power of social publishers, to get the right audience to your content. All my experiences have taught me a lot and now I want to share that knowledge with you. You can find me at Jeremiahboehner.com where I write about content marketing, life hacking, and entrepreneurship. You can also reach me at Mylikes if you want to discuss getting more traffic to your Blog. Jeremiah@Mylikes.com

66 Ways to Discover New Blog Topics

1. **Your Life**:

Use tools like Evernote and the voice recorder on your phone to capture moments of inspiration as they come to you. You'll be surprised how things that may seem mundane will spark something creative. Often the best idea's come from your hobbies and passions. Your content will be better when you choose to write about things you are already knowledgeable about. Even if you think people won't be interested, you might be surprised. The world is a big place.

2. **Look at the Problems You're Facing:**

Whether it be your health, life, relationships, career, money, etc. Writing about the problems you're dealing with and how you overcome them, will help you connect with your readers. There is always someone out there who is facing the same struggle, or someone who will face that struggle in the future, no matter how unique you think the problem is. Why not share your struggles and successes with your readers? Connect on a personal level.

3. **Watch the News:**

Watching the news is always a good idea, in order to be aware of what is going on in the world, and the community around you. It will also help you discover niche topics that people care about, find a unique angle or position to take on the subjects they cover and you'll be good to go.

4. **TV Shows and Documentaries:**

This will give you an endless supply of subjects to talk about. If you can, find a way to combine your industry and a current popular TV show, and you'll be generating great relevant content.

(Examples: How to get Arms like Spartacus, Lessons Learned from Breaking Bad about Entrepreneurship, What Tim Allen taught me About Being a Dad, Leadership Lessons from Star Trek TNG.)

5. **Amazon.com:**

The world's largest online retailer is also a one of the world largest search engines. You can use tools like Merchant Words to get the search volume of items on Amazon. If you can find some way to incorporate those items into your blogging you might see an uptick in search traffic. Also be sure to check out their 'best selling' feature for what's currently popular.

6. **Clickbank:**

Clickbank.com is the largest affiliate marketplace on the web. They sell a wide variety of products. Like Amazon you'll want to see what's selling best, as there will be a lot of people talking about those products and topics. There are other places like JVzoo.com, Share a Sale, and Commission Junction that you should also check out.

7. **StumbleUpon:**

StumbleUpon is a site people visit to 'stumble' across interesting content, based on their interests. Post whatever you write to the site, and also use it to search what other people are doing, and gain some inspiration.

8. **Yahoo!'s Trending:**

Yahoo! may not be the search engine powerhouse it once was but it is still a major content producer and curator. Check out their trending section on the homepage.

9. **Twitter:**

Current news often breaks first on Twitter. It can be a great resource to find trending topics to discuss on your blog. Creating lists of influencers for your industry will make your searches easier. Tools like followerwonk and buzzsumo can help you find the top influencers in your niche.

10. **Google Trends:**
Google Trends shows information on what people are currently searching for. You can do general searches or browse by category. Each category will be useful in helping you find more info about what readers want to know.

11. **Magazines:**
Magazines may not be the mighty empire they once were, and many have made their way to the web, however they can still be a treasure trove of well-researched topics. You can look at their distribution numbers to get a better idea of their reach, and this will help you assess the popularity of any given magazine. You can also pick up old copies to repurpose old ideas from the past.

12. **Technorati:**
Technorati is a blog aggregator. You can search for top blogs in your industry and by category.

13. **ComScore:**

ComScore provides insights into markets and industries. It is often used for measuring a site's authority in a specific industry or category, for the sake of purchasing advertising. Sites with a high Comscore are often highly visited and have a strong authority in their space.

14. **Google Suggest:**

You know when you type something in to Google, and just like an over-eager boyfriend or girlfriend it tries to finish your sentence? That's all it takes to find out what Google would suggest. Just start typing in a topic, and see what the search engine comes up with. Use tools like MOZ to see what links come up in the number one rank. Take a look at the site, and brainstorm how you might be able to beat that rank.

15. **Google Keyword Planner:**

Used to find popular keywords. You can either give it a general keyword and ask it to generate a list of similar words (a good way to find subtopics,) or you can enter a website URL and see what keywords it is ranking for.

16. **LongTailPro:**

Long tail keywords are words that people use when they are searching for something very specific. It is easier to get ranked with long tail keywords, and they can help you drive a lot of revenue via ads or product sales. LongTailPro is an advanced keyword tool that will help you find the search volume and competitiveness of keywords in your industry. It does the same thing that Google Keyword Search does, but focuses on long tail keywords instead.

17. **Ubersuggest**

Ubersuggest is another great, free keyword search engine.

18. **AOL:**

Once the dominating internet service provider across the entire digital landscape, it has since transitioned into a media empire similar to Yahoo! Their homepage has a lot of trending stories that can help spark your ideas. Check out AOL and see what you find.

19. **Delicious:**

Delicious is a social bookmarking tool that was originally created to allow you to access your bookmarks from different devices. It now shows popular bookmarks from around the globe, so you can see what other people are bookmarking. Many influencers on Twitter and Facebook have links to their Delicious profiles. Check them out to see what they are consuming.

20. **43Things:**
43 Things is a neat little community where people list things they would like to do. You can use it to see problems people are having, and different things they would like to do, and then you can write about them.

21. **BuzzFeed:**
BuzzFeed is a modern-day mecca for popular and profitable ideas. They are always updating their site with 'buzzing' topics, and trending subjects.
www.buzzfeed.com

22. **Listverse:**
Listverse is a site that pumps out 'top 10' lists in almost every category you can think of, daily. There are a lot of potential blog post ideas here. You can take a list that's been made and expand on it, or maybe you think their list is all wrong and want to create your own.

23. **Reddit:**

Reddit calls itself the "front page of the internet," and has thousands of 'subreddits,' that you can browse through to get ideas. This is a great way to find out what the most popular topics are in current events. Reddit is also good for distributing your content. Keep in mind: they do have some strong anti-spam rules, so make sure you comply, and participate instead of just posting articles.

24. **Craigslist:**

You never know what you will find on Craigslist. Browsing through the categories, and subcategories is an excellent way to search for topics and ideas.

25. **Wikipedia:**

You can find everything on Wikipedia, literally. Go search and browse your heart out. You are bound to find something that sparks an idea in its archives. If you see an article that is lacking a source for a topic you specialize in, use it as an opportunity to submit your own links and content. As long as it is well researched, you may get some high quality linkbacks.

26. **YouTube Keyword Searches:**

Millions of hours of videos are uploaded to YouTube every day, on every imaginable topic.

You will know if a certain category is popular because there will be a lot of different videos covering it. Julie Joyce of Search Engine Land suggests taking favorable words from the YouTube keyword tool, and then inserting them with "exact match" into both YouTube's search engine, as well as Google's (to be extra thorough). You can even embed really good videos on your own page, with a brief summary to help boost traffic.

27. **Listal:**

Listal is similar to Listverse. It contains tons of lists about anything and everything you could imagine. See the potential here? Read a few and you are bound to come up with something!

28. **HowStuffWorks:**

Howstuffworks is an awesome site to learn information on things you don't really know much about. If there is a topic on here, it usually means there is a demand for it and people want to know about it. This is a great, quick way to become an expert. Some of the stuff on there is pretty dryly written so if you can find a way to make "how hot dogs are made" interesting, gross, or funny, then you'll strike internet gold.

29. **WikiHow:**

WikiHow is another one of those sites that explains how to do almost anything, and everything. Browse through the various topics and see what people are reading. You can even see things that Wikihow needs help with and you can submit your content in an attempt to get linkbacks to your site.

30. **Fiverr.com:**

Fiverr is currently one of the most popular sites and market places on the internet. Simply looking at what people are selling, and browsing through the categories will give you hundreds of ideas of articles you can write for your own site. Here's one that will give you 25 Original Blog Topic Ideas.

31. **About:**

Remember how we said that where there is a need for knowledge there is a great topic? About.com is another site where people go to learn. A few minutes browsing through the topics will reveal a lot of potential ideas.

32. **Yahoo! Answers:**

Yahoo! Answers has millions of questions people are asking. It is likely that there are many more people out there who want to know the same answer. Questions highlight potential problems people have, and your site can be the solution. This can also be a great source to distribute your content. When you find questions that you've already answered on your site you can post a response linking to your blog.

33. **Quora:**
Quora is another question and answer site. This is where people tend to go with their more 'intelligent' questions, and is a great way to find topics that target a different category of people. Like Yahoo! Answers, this is a great resources for distributing your content and establishing yourself as an expert in an area. So when you respond to questions, and want to link back to your site, make sure to do it in a thoughtful and non-spammy way.

34. **Rebel Mouse:**
Rebel Mouse allows users to syndicate content from different websites and social channels around the web. There are tons of useful hubs of information on this site, and plenty of opportunity to find a good topic or two.

35. **Udemy:**
Udemy is a digital marketplace for courses about everything. This is a great place to find out popular topics. It can be a treasure trove

of information for how-to articles. Also if you've already written extensively about a topic, turn it into a course and either give it away for free, or make a little money.

36. **Lynda:**
Like Udemy Lynda.com is another online learning resource. Unlike Udemy, users can gain access to the courses by subscribing for a membership to the site, instead of purchasing on a course-by-course basis. You will be able to view the popular courses, without actually having to pay for the actual material.

37. **Ehow:**
Ehow is a hub of information on a wide variety of topics. It is really useful in helping you identify potential blog ideas. You can always watch the site's videos, and write summaries of them for people who don't want to take the time to watch for themselves.

38. **Kindle Marketplace:**
Browse through the Amazon e-book marketplace. Which books are selling well? These are popular markets for you to try to enter. Take these ideas over to one of the keyword sites we have mentioned, and voila, you've found your topic.

39. **Alexa:**

Alexa lists popular websites and their ranking. Enter sites into the search bar for the industry you're trying to cover and see how the sites rank.

40. **LinkedIn Groups:**

LinkedIn Groups are little communities that gather around topics and industries. Find different groups in your market and start connecting with people. A lot of the groups are filled with spam, but there are also a lot of people who ask questions, and are looking for advice or resources. You can even start your own group as a way to grow your network and influence.

41. **Ask:**

Ask.com used to be one of the Top search engines on the planet before Google came along and knocked everyone out. Today, it is still a great resource for finding answers to quick questions.

42. **Pinterest:**

Pinterest is quickly becoming a huge traffic driver for blogs. People only 'pin' things that they find important or entertaining. Search for the topic you are thinking of writing about, and browse through the pictures of what people are interested in. This will give you an idea of what is popular for those categories. Connect with popular pinners and get them to share your stuff and guest post on your blog for a boost in traffic.

43. **Tumblr:**

Tumblr is a blogging platform with over 90,000,000 different sites. Browsing through the categories will bring up a lot of potential ideas.

44. **Flickr:**

Flickr is a hub for photographers to share their work. What are people taking pictures of? You know what they say... "A picture is worth 1,000 words." There are some really great blog ideas just waiting to be discovered over there.

45. **Instagram:**

Ignore the selfies, Instagram is filled with them, but it is also one of the most popular social channels in the world, right now. You are bound to find some interesting topics and products featured there.

46. **Dailymotion**

This site is similar to YouTube, but a little more obscure. Check out the videos there for some more ideas.

www.dailymotion.com

47. **Slideshare**

Slideshare curates a lot of interesting slideshows. The most popular slides on display are the topics people are most interested in. Industry leaders from all over the world upload slides, and it can be a great resource to find information for your blog. You can even turn your own articles into slide decks, and share them there.

48. **Photobucket:**

People use Photobucket to share pictures with their friends. What are people uploading? Which photos get the most ratings? Take a look at what is popular there and see if anything inspires you to write a great article.

49. **Piratebay:**

Piratebay is the infamous torrenting site where people go to download illegal copies of movies and other digital media. Check out what's popular over there to see if there's something you can write about. It can also be a great way to distribute an e-book you're giving away for free.

50. **Bing:**

A lot of people tend to forget about Bing with Google around, but this search engine is a great alternative. It is always good to search and see if you get different results. Use their Keyword search to see what people are looking for.

51. **DeviantArt:**

DeviantArt is a site for people to share art and graphics-- checkout what is trending over there. Popular sites like Buzzfeed usually use DevianArt to find interesting images, and then they add some text and share them with their followers. You can see an example here.

52. **Likes:**

Likes is an up and coming social media network where people upload their favorite images, gifs, and galleries. See what images are popular and how you might be able to put your spin on them.

53. **Mylikes:**

MyLikes is an advertising platform that will help you distribute your content across the social web. Upload your content and set your budget, then watch your visitors grow. Be sure to optimize your posts for social sharing to get the maximum results from your campaign.

54. **Yelp:**
Yelp.com lets you check out local businesses and their customer reviews. What is popular? This is an excellent idea for people who want to feature local businesses on their site. You can also use Yelp to find popular local businesses for articles like this one.

55. **Google Plus:**
Google Plus is often an overlooked resource for inspiration and distribution. Take a look at what your friends are sharing (sometimes unbeknownst to them) and see what catches your eye. It might also be worth trying to build a following on Google Plus, less players in the game means it's easier to build a following.

56. **Meetup:**
A site that lists real-life meetups in your neighborhood, based off a wide variety of different subjects. People are usually pretty passionate about a topic if they are willing to meet up in person to talk about it. Passion= a profitable topic. This can also be an opportunity to expand your influence offline, as a lot of event organizers are looking for people to speak at their meetups.

57. **Tribe**

Tribe allows people to build communities or "tribes" with other bloggers and social media experts within their niche. Once you have found your topic, join a tribe and find other people to collaborate with.

58. **Buzzsumo**

Buzzsumo is a great tool, available in both free and paid versions. It allows you to search for popular blog articles based on their social sharing, as well as influencers. Type in a topic like "Air Jordans" and see what comes up. You can put your own spin on already popular content, then reach out to the influencers and share your content with them.

59. **Read Comments:**

Expert blogger Murray Newlands recommends looking at the comments in your articles to see what questions people are asking. You can also use Buzzsumo to look at the comments of other popular articles to see what people are saying over there, and hopefully find some inspiration.

60. **Blog Topic Generators:**

Hubspot has been created a topic generator. All your need to do is enter 3 nouns and it spits out several different ideas. Portent also has one that gives you reasons for the topic they gave you.

Content Forest also has a basic one that's free. TweakyourBiz This tools gives you a plethora of blog topic ideas by combining popular keywords and your topic. Some are gold and others are garbage but it's worth checking out.

61. **Read this post and do all the idea's here.**

62. **AllTop**

AllTop collects top headlines from the latest stories and best blogs around the web. Using Alltop can allow you to quickly scan what's popular on different social networks without having to jump back and forth.

63. **Practice Free Association**

Free association is a technique created by Sigmund Freud, which is often used to uncover suppressed feelings, and it can also be used for coming up with blog topics. This might best to do with a friend or a writing partner. You start off with one idea and shout out the first thing that comes to mind. Keep doing that till you feel done. I suggest using a voice recorder to capture all your ideas.

64. **Client Case Studies**

Blogging expert Hunter Boyle recommends taking a look at client case studies and seeing what you can glean from those. Often case studies are jam-packed with lots of interesting facts and information but the average person doesn't want to sift through all that data to find the nuggets of insight. Save your readers time by doing a thoughtful summary and they'll keep coming back for more.

65. **Interviews**

You don't need to conduct interviews with industry leaders to gain great insights and materials for your blog. Take a look at interviews they've already done and take the things they've said around a certain subject and compile into a list of thoughtful quotes and insights. For example if you have fitness blog and want to interview the Rock, just look at all his interviews and see where he talks about fitness and compile that into a summary. Want to interview Richard Branson about entrepreneurship? He's done plenty of speeches and interviews about it, find the gems from each one and put that together.

66. **Reach Out to Customers/Readers**

You always want to ask your readers and customers what questions they have, or what they'd like to learn. Keep a running list of these questions so you'll always have a pool of resources to draw from.

More Tools for Bloggers

1. Stay Focused (Google Chrome):
The free StayFocusd app (available on Chrome only) is a must-have for any blogger who finds themselves distracted by all that internet has to offer. It allows you block sites that you know are a distraction for. You set the amount of time you want to spend on any given site per day, and it will give shut you down after the limit. A lot of people use it for blocking social media sites during their peak creativity times so they can focus on their writing.

2. SumoMe:
SumoMe is a great host of free and paid tools for all bloggers. It has an excellent e-mail collection tool that will integrate with all the major e-mail platforms. It also has a click-to-tweet tool that is pretty handy, and a host of other valuable services. Check it out if you haven't already.

3. Easy Pricing Tables:
Created by Fat Cat Apps, Easy Pricing Tables allows you to easily create pricing tables on Wordpress. Their system is really simple, and allows you to create pricing tables without any technical knowledge. Each license comes with 5 different designs and over 300 icons you can use on your site. It's also mobile responsive which is key if you want to keep your customers happy as more and more e-commerce is conducted via mobile phones.

4. **Namechk:**

One of the first things you want to do when you start a new site, is make sure that all the different social media channels are available. Well Namechk takes care of that for you. It allows you to check the availability of the desired URL names on all social platforms at once.

5. **Easel.ly:**

Easel.ly allows those of us without much creativity to make beautiful infographics, using pre-created templates. Users can customize their infographics simply by dragging and dropping objects from within the platform.

6. **99designs**:

99designs is like an eBay for graphic design work. You can list your project and budget on the platform and 100's of designers will submit ideas for it. This gives you a wide variety of options without the risk of paying a designer to find out after the fact, that you hate what they came up with. Tim Ferris, Author of the *4Hr Work Week* and other "4Hr" series uses this services to design all of his book covers.

7. **Wistia:**

Wistia allows you to host videos and embed them on your site without eating up your server bandwidth, or having to worry about YouTube trolls commenting all over your videos. It supports iPad/iPhones, video analytics, social sharing, customization of video players, video heat maps and more. This service is great if you want to create some special members-only videos that you don't want to upload to YouTube. The customization features really add a professional polish to your videos. One of the best tools is the ability to insert a 'call to action,' such as a way for users to subscribe to your email list from within the video. Now that's something YouTube can't do.

8. **Buffer App:**

Buffer App allows you to pre-schedule tweets, Facebook posts, LinkedIn post, etc., relatively easy. The tool even has a learning feature that will automatically share your content when it detects that it will get the most engagement.

9. **HootSuite:**

Like Buffer, Hootsuite makes it easy to manage multiple accounts from one fairly easy-to-use template. There is a small subscription fee, but it's been around for a while and is a widely used platform.

10. **Topsy:**

Like Buzzsumo, Topsy.com allows you to search the social web for various topics and influencers. You can search for people who are tweeting about your subject and reach out to them with your story. They have a great free version and a great paid version as well, for those of you needing something more robust.

11. **Dragon Dictation:**

Dragon Dictation is arguably one of the best auto-dictation softwares out there. If you're like me, and sitting down to write a 5,000 word blog post seems like a pain in the ass, but talking about that subject for an hour or two is no problem, you might want to check out this software. Here's what one happy Amazon customer had to say about it:

> I was able to install Dragon Naturally Speaking Premium on a computer running Windows 7 without incident. The program includes a microphone that worked well. I had several family members try the program, including two young teens, and all were able to quickly and easily produce text. Although the text wasn't error-free, the accuracy was still very impressive. There were few mistakes, and suggested alternatives made sense.
>
> I was interested in how well this would work for one of my children who has ADHD and is often frustrated with the mechanics of writing. I can see the ease of Dragon as one less barrier to overcome when crafting a paper, and I think it will be helpful to her.
>
> My husband used his IT experience to devise a creative test for the program to approximate real-world conditions. He inserted profanity within the commands themselves (not in the text) and was amused that the program went about its business in the normal way, totally ignoring everything but the command. So if you get frustrated, you can feel free to tell the program to start an #$% paragraph with total confidence.

Dragon was also able to handle computer commands like opening a file or browser (we tested on Firefox). Bottom line: Dragon does what it claims to be able to do, and it does it very well."

12. **Evernote:**

Evernote is a cloud-based note taking system that everyone loves. It allows you to easily create and share notes with multiple people. Like Google Drive, Evernote can be accessed from all of your devices, and unlike Google Drive it's easy to use from a mobile device. It also allows you work on notes when you're not connected to the internet and it will then sync your notes when you reconnect. Evernote Web Clipper allows you to clip from the web and save directly to your Evernote account.
Price: Free, premium starts at $5/month or $45 dollars a year.

13. **DropBox:**

DropBox is a virtual hard drive that you can install on your desktop and mobile devices. It allows for easy sharing of files across devices, and will sync the files across all platforms, to keep them up-to-date. You can use Dropbox on your mobile device, your desktop, or via the web. The Pro version allows for up to one terabyte of data to be stored, and many other features you can check out here.
Price: Free 2GB+ Pro is $9.99 a month or $99 a year.

14. **Last Pass:**

Last Pass is a password management tool, which can be used on most devices. It remembers all your different passwords, which can be a huge blessing when you have several different accounts that you can't keep straight. You just need to install the software on your browser and your computer, and Last Pass does the rest. They have a mobile app for iPhones and Android devices.
Price: Free, They offer a premium version for $12 a year.

15. **The Hemingway App:**

The Hemingway App is a web-based tool that helps you make your writing easier to understand, and highlights common errors.
Price: Web Version is free, there is a desktop version for $7.

16. **Grammarly:**

Grammarly is an online tool that proofreads your content. It finds common grammar and spelling errors, as well as checks your content against plagiarism.
Price: $29.95/month.

17. **WPCurve:**

WPCurve is a great service for people who are running their blogs on Wordpress, but lack the technical skills to make minor, but important, adjustments. They offer a variety of services and can often fix your problem in less than 24hrs. Need

help installing a landing page? No problem! Want to make your site hacker proof? No problem!
Price: Plans start at $69 dollars a month, and goes up to $99 a month.

18. **Sweet Process:**

Sweet Process is a tool that will allow you to systemize your daily blog tasks so you can outsource them. This will allow you to free up your time so you can focus on creating content. What type of systems can you create? Anything! Systemize your social media sharing, your influencer outreach, or your research process!
Price: $19 a month all the way to $99 a month.

19. **Assistant.to:**

Assistant.to is a free Gmail plugin that makes it super easy to schedule meetings. I use it everyday at work, and it's made the back and forth of finding a time that works to meet disappear. I just send it a list of times that I'm available to chat and the other person picks a time that works best, then both our calendars are updated.
Price: Free

20. **Bubblews:**

Bubblews is a newer platform on the web. It is a blogging platform that allows users to upload short blog posts on any given topic, and actually earn money for the traffic that their post receives. Users earn a little bit of money each time someone clicks on, or likes their post. You can cash out once you get up to $50 in the "bank." This is a great place to

find new ideas you may have never heard of before. Surf the platform, find an interesting topic, do your own research, and expand on it. You can create your own account online at Bubblews.com.
Price: Free

21. **Skimmin:**
"Skimmin" is the easiest way for busy people to stay up-to-date with current events. If you aren't sure what is happening in the world and need some ideas for "trending" content, download the app to your smartphone and sign up. "Skimmin" for a couple of days, and see what you find. You are sure to find something to write about.
Price: Free

22. **Snapchat Discover:**
I know what you may be thinking, "Really!? You're suggesting I use Snapchat?" Well the thing is, they just launched this new platform called "Discover," and it's actually pretty cool. Various news and entertainment sources, such as *CNN*, *Comedy Central*, and several more upload trending content onto their own Snapchat story, daily. This is a really great, fun, and exciting way for you to find new content on a wide variety of different topics. Download it to your smartphone or tablet and check it regularly to stay up-to-date on the latest and greatest in current events.
Price: Free

23. **Byline:**

This is an app that allows you to read all of the latest updates from your favorite sources in one place. It even syncs with your Google reader account. Many writers use this to keep up with current events, and to spark inspiration for new ideas to write about on their own site. Download it and give it a try! You are sure to find a new idea from this platform.
Price: Free

24. **CoverItLive:**

This platform allows users to easily cover live events, in real-time. Chances are, you are going to come across a time in your writing career when you want to be able to cover an event live, and easily be able to upload your work. You probably would rather do this without having to carry a bulky computer or tablet around. Now all you have to do is download this app on your phone, and you're good to go! This app allows you to do it all, whether you want to upload audio or video, simple status updates, or even send out emails with links to the events. We think it is definitely worth checking out.
Price: Free

25. **Google Alerts:**

Set up some Google alerts with a few keywords having to do with your niche. Have the platform

Free Blog Topics Download!
Not Very Creative or just looking for a list of go to type of articles? Go to http://www.jeremiahboehner.com/content-ideas-for-businesses/ and enter your e-mail and you'll get a free download of over 35 Blog Topics you can use on your blog right away and get Jeremiah Boehner. More Than 60 Ultra Hot Resources to Help You Develop Kick-Butt Idea's For Your Blog!